NATIONAL
GEOGRAPHIC

A HOMESTEADING
COMMUNITY
of the 1880s

GARE THOMPSON

Produced through the worldwide resources of the National Geographic
Society, John M. Fahey, Jr., President and Chief Executive Officer;
Gilbert M. Grosvenor, Chairman of the Board; Nina D. Hoffman,
Executive Vice President and President, Books and School Publishing.

PREPARED BY NATIONAL GEOGRAPHIC SCHOOL PUBLISHING
Ericka Markman, Senior Vice President; Steve Mico, Editorial Director;
Marianne Hiland, Editorial Manager; Anita Schwartz, Project Editor; Tara
Peterson, Editorial Assistant; Jim Hiscott, Design Manager; Linda
McKnight, Art Director; Diana Bourdrez, Anne Whittle, Photo Research;
Matt Wascavage, Manager of Publishing Services; Sean Philpotts,
Production Coordinator; Jane Ponton, Production Artist.

Production: Clifton M. Brown III, Manufacturing and Quality Control.

CONSULTANT REVIEWER
Dr. Russell L. Adams, Professor and Chair
Department of Afro-American Studies
Howard University

PROGRAM DEVELOPMENT
Gare Thompson Associates, Inc.

BOOK DESIGN
Inkwell Publishing Solutions, Inc.

Published by the National Geographic Society
1145 17th Street, N.W.
Washington, D.C. 20036-4688

ISBN: 0-7922-8680-4

Sixth Printing July, 2004
Printed in Canada.

TABLE OF CONTENTS

CHAPTER 1
Sharecroppers No More!
Leaving Georgetown, Kentucky, 1877 5

CHAPTER 2
The Promised Land
Arriving in Nicodemus, Kansas, 1878 8

CHAPTER 3
Nicodemus Grows
Celebrating Our Community, 1881 14

CHAPTER 4
The Dream Comes True
Boomtown, 1887. 18

EPILOGUE
The Dream Fades
Still Our Home, 1888 22

GLOSSARY 24

SHARECROPPERS NO MORE!

Leaving Georgetown, Kentucky, 1877

My name is Mary Lewis. I'm 12. I've been picking tobacco for as long as I can remember. I'd rather go to school. Every day Ma tells me that I'm smart.

My whole family works in the tobacco fields. We don't own them. Mr. James does. He lives in a big house. He used to own us. We're **sharecroppers**. Pa has to share half of what we grow with him. The crops are poor this year. We won't make but a few dollars. Pa says with six mouths to feed, times will be hard. Things don't seem that different from when we were slaves.

We live at the end of a dirt road. The other field-workers live near us. We're close to the fields but far from town. Our house is two small rooms. In winter, the cabin is always cold. But it's home.

In the tobacco fields, we can hear people chanting, "Free land. Free land in Kansas." Inside church, men give talks about Kansas. They call it the "promised land."

Every day Pa and Ma talk about Kansas. Maybe in Kansas I can go to school longer than two months. I'd like that. The people leaving are called **Exodusters.** They're called this because they are leaving, or making an exodus, from their home.

My Uncle John heard "Pap" Singleton talk in Tennessee. "Pap" is an ex-slave. He helps people like us move to Kansas. Uncle John heard that the land is good in Kansas. In church, we heard about Nicodemus, Kansas. It's a town just for freed slaves.

Even George Washington, my nine-year-old brother, talks about Kansas. When he's running errands for the postmaster, he hears talk about Kansas. I wonder if Kansas will be as beautiful and green as Kentucky. I'd miss the rolling hills and clear brooks, but not the tobacco. Pa keeps saying, "Our own land. Our land."

In the fall, we sell our crops. We get only seven dollars. It is not enough for Kansas. We need five dollars to join the group going this spring. We need money for the train to Ellis, Kansas. Pa says that he'll work as a carpenter this winter. Ma will do washing. I'll help her. The boys will work, too.

Finally by spring we have enough money. We will keep some money to buy a horse and a plow in Kansas. Most of the families in our church are going. We will travel from Georgetown to Ellis and then on to Nicodemus.

We have little to pack—some pots, our clothes, and Ma's Bible. We write all our family history in it. Our group is leaving today. Mr. James, who owned our land, was mad, but we are still going. Our church glows in the morning sun. It is a good sign. We begin our journey. Our minister leads us. We sing as we leave.

We take the train to Ellis. There, some people get sick. Ma says they have measles. We have to stay in tents. We can't go anywhere until everyone is better. Some children die. Ma prays. George Washington has a fever, but he gets better. Finally we begin the walk to Nicodemus, our new home.

▲ **Benjamin "Pap" Singleton**

CHAPTER 2

THE PROMISED LAND

Arriving in Nicodemus, Kansas, 1878

At Ellis, some families turn back. Others stay in Ellis. We decide to go on. With just a **compass** to guide us, we set out for Nicodemus on foot. We follow paths made by Native Americans and buffalo. There are no roads.

We are happy to be on our way to the "promised land." By day we travel along the dusty paths. As we get closer to Nicodemus, the land begins to look like a desert. People already miss the green hills of Kentucky. The dream of owning land keeps us going. At night we eat around a campfire. Ma is the best cook in the group. Men fire shots in the air to scare away animals. We sleep on the hard, cold ground and dream of our land. We've been on the road for a week.

Finally, we arrive at Nicodemus. But where is the town? We see many holes with smoke rising from them. People come out of the holes, or **dugouts**. The dugouts are their homes. They greet us, the new **homesteaders,** or settlers. Welcome to Nicodemus!

Surely this is not the "promised land." I know Ma wants to cry, but she doesn't. She smiles at Pa. He smiles back. "Well, we will own the land!" he says. We all set up tents. We'll live in them until we have our land.

We're lucky. The first settlers often had only a hoe to farm with, no money, and few seeds. We have seeds to plant corn. Pa has money for a horse and a plow, too.

The people tell us we have come at the right time, spring. Spring is the time to plant. The early settlers arrived too late to plant last year. The winter months were hard. Some friendly Osage Indians gave them food. The settlers made it through the winter. Things will be better this year, they said. I hope so.

Today Pa paid five dollars for our land. He bought it from Mr. Hill, whose company founded Nicodemus. We now own a farm. It is outside Nicodemus. Pa and Ma are so proud. We are landowners! We work for ourselves now!

Hundreds of people have moved to Nicodemus. We all help each other. Pa, my brothers, and some other men walk to Ellis. They are going to buy a horse and a plow. We will share the horse and plow with our neighbors. Some of the men work in Ellis. Other than farming, there are no jobs in Nicodemus.

Ma told me that Mrs. Fletcher teaches school in her dugout. I can go this fall. We will work on our farm until then.

Our house will be made out of **sod,** or soil. We will cut large squares of sod to build the house. It will be better than a dugout. There are few trees so there is no wood.

We all use sod. I am learning to gather buffalo chips, sunflowers, and cottonwood for fuel. George Washington and the other boys find buffalo bones to sell. They get $6.00 a ton!

I miss Main Street in Georgetown. Here we have only dirt paths. Our Main Street has one small general store. We call the general store, "generally out of everything." Most of the time we find little to buy. Few people have money anyway. We have little left. But the people want to build up the town.

The land is dry here. Our neighbor tells us it is wetter than last summer. Last summer crops were poor, and many of the animals died. Pa wants to plant more than corn. We hope it rains.

We all work hard planting. We're up at dawn, and we work until dark. Then we do the same the next day. Somehow the work feels different. Maybe it's because this land is ours.

Our minister wants to build a church. Pa and the boys will help. Soon we will have a place to gather and talk. It will be like our old church. With good crops, more people will come here. Then we'll build more stores. Soon our town will be big and successful like the towns back east.

CHAPTER 3

NICODEMUS GROWS

Celebrating Our Community, 1881

Three years have passed and our farm has grown. We now own 100 acres of land. We work hard to grow crops. Ma works as a cook in a hotel. I go to school. My younger brothers work on the farm. Charles, the oldest, works on the railroad at Ellis. Sometimes he comes home to help on the farm. Nicodemus is our home.

We work on our farm from sunrise to sunset. The crops are good this year. We have cows and hogs, too. The hogs are funny. They eat old corn and any leftover food we have.

George Washington names each hog. His favorite is Benjamin Franklin. I don't have the heart to tell him that they will all be gone by fall. Pa says we'll buy more.

I like our sod house. Of course, when it rains, the whole house gets wet. Bugs and mice find their way in. Still, it's better than a dugout. Our neighbors built a wooden house. Pa says if our crops are good, maybe we can build one, too. Wood is hard to find here. And it costs a lot.

Slowly, our little town grows. Over 600 people now live in the Nicodemus area. Farmers raise hogs and cattle as well as corn and wheat. Some farmers even grow rice corn, a new crop that comes from Egypt. Farmers still share horses and mules, but there are more animals than before.

Inside a neighbor's wooden house ▼

Main Street has a post office. Z. T. Fletcher, who founded the first general store, is postmaster. There's three general stores, three hotels, two stables, and a drugstore. Nicodemus has become a successful town. I like living here now.

The best part of living here is school. We have a new stone school. We go to school from November to March. There are 45 children. I help teach the younger ones. I teach them their letters and how to count. I read them stories.

Our teacher, Mrs. Fletcher, says that I've really been a big help to her. We don't have many books here. I know most of the stories by heart. Pa says we have the best school in Kansas. I think so, too.

I miss my brother Charles. He says he likes working as a **porter**, carrying people's bags at the Ellis railroad station. I know he misses home. Pa tells Charles to save his money. Then he can buy the land next to us. Charles wants to farm. I want to teach or do something that's not farming. I like our farm, but I like books better.

Pa says Nicodemus is growing fast. Ma says many people stay at the hotel. They can get a bed and a good dinner for 50 cents. Ma says it's a good deal.

Nicodemus is a big town now. It has wooden houses and stores. We can walk down Main Street and shop.

Mrs. Fletcher, our teacher, opened a hat store. I have been working in her store. Women buy hats to wear to church and for special days. We put ribbons, flowers, and even birds on the hats. Ma says a big hat is a good hat. We make them in all sizes.

Pa says we should be proud of our town. We sure were during **Emancipation** Day. On that day we celebrated our being freed from slavery. It was a fine celebration. I wore a hat with pretty ribbons that Mrs. Fletcher made just for me. We're going to have an Emancipation Day every year.

Almost a thousand people came to Nicodemus to celebrate Emancipation Day. We ate ham, corn, and biscuits. Ma made pecan pies and sold them. They were all gone in about an hour! George Washington won a ribbon for his hog, Benjamin Franklin. Pa says he can keep him. George Washington was happy. He smiled all day long.

Charles came down from Ellis. He says he has heard that the railroad is coming to Nicodemus. Pa says if it does, the town will really grow. We all hope the railroad comes.

CHAPTER 4

THE DREAM COMES TRUE

Boomtown, 1887

Nine years have passed since we first came to Nicodemus. It is 1887. People are now calling Nicodemus a **boomtown.** It has grown and is richer than before. Crops have been good for the past six years. Plenty of rain has fallen. Nicodemus is one of the most successful towns in Graham County. The town elects leaders for the **county.** These leaders help to run the state of Kansas. We are proud of our town.

Baptist church

The town has four general stores, a grocery and two drugstores. There are three land companies, two large hotels, two stables, and a boot repair shop. New churches have been built. We have a doctor, a lawyer, and a **blacksmith.** There are jobs in Nicodemus. We have newspapers, too.

I, Mary Lewis, am now a teacher. We have the largest school in our county. Our school is a new four-room building. Two of us teach the children. School now lasts from September to June. The children want to learn, but many still have to farm. They find it hard to study and work, but they do both.

A limestone ▼ house

Charles has moved back home. He works as a stone **mason.** Now most of our buildings are made of stone. He also builds fences and chimneys. He has a small farm next to ours. He still loves farming, but he earns more money doing stonework.

My little brother Robert is my student. It is funny to teach him. He won't sit still and wants to be home with his animals. I tell him he can't bring pets to school, but somehow they follow him and wait outside. He likes science. I'm hoping he'll be a doctor.

We now have a sidewalk on Main Street. No more dirt paths. We have stores with front porches, too. Pa and the other farmers like to stand there and talk. Sometimes I think they talk more than they buy.

THE NICODEMUS CYCLONE

Nicodemus, Graham County, Kansas, Friday. July 20, 1888.

Vol. 3, No. 10.

J. E. PORTER, Editor and Proprietor.

OUR MOTTO:—FAITHFUL TO OUR FRIENDS AND GENEROUS TO OUR FOES.

ONLY ONE DOLLAR A YEAR.

THE SAME OLD STORY.

There are things of which the recurrence may be predicted with safety; with the summer solstice the burlesque, with the autumn the fruit, with winter the snow, and with the Presidential campaign the Southern outrage.

It is the same old story over and over again, whether it be told of a county in Mississippi or Tennessee or of a parish in Louisiana. A paragraph may be written in 1888, leaving names of persons and places blank, and in 1902 it will be historically true by mere insertion of names. It might run thus: "The county of —— in the State of —— is one of the black districts, the colored population outnumbering the white by at least four to one. By means of corruption best known to the leaders, the majority has actually succeeded in electing its candidates during the off years of politics, so that the county offices were occupied by colored people. This

The Leavenworth Standard refuses to hoist the democratic ticket. The ticket headed by Judge Martin is too respectable for the short haired crowd and they can't swallow it. Several of the river counties have openly revolted. This action shows the real animus of democracy. The only time they have a set of clean candidates, discord reigns rampant. We are sorry to see it, not that it will effect in the least the big majority D. R. Anthony or any other nominee of the republican party will get, but because there is no credit in slugging a set of drunkards. We want our man to beat a respectable democrat. John Martin has encountered a big job in leading the faithful this time, for they are well aware of the fact that the fight for state officers is love's labor lost only so far as it gives them favor with the administration.

The democratic press of the country is already explaining that they are not in favor of free trade. The

▲ The *Nicodemus Cyclone* was the town's last newspaper.

I also write for our local paper, the *Nicodemus Cyclone*. I write about the festivals, celebrations, and other events in town.

I write about what a good town Nicodemus is. We even have our own bank. The town has plenty of land, the Solomon River, and jobs. The bigger the town gets, the better life will be for all of us.

Pa, Charles, and others in town talk about the railroad all the time. We must get the railroad to pass through town. Without it, new people and businesses will have no reason to come here. We need the railroad for more jobs, to ship goods, and to bring people to visit our town. Pa and some others are getting together to meet with the railroad people. I hope they are successful.

Three railroads might come to Nicodemus. They are the *Missouri,* the *Union,* and the *Santa Fe.* We have to raise money to pay for building the railroad. We have voted to do this. Now we wait.

All through this long, hot summer we have waited for news. We finally hear from the *Missouri* in September. I am in school when the news hits. The *Missouri* has turned us down. Their railroad will go to Colorado. We are all disappointed, but maybe the *Union* or the *Santa Fe* will come here.

We will not know about the other two railroads until next year. All we can do now is hope. Some people think the railroads will come. Others think they won't. I'm not sure.

I ask Pa what will happen if the railroads don't come. Pa shakes his head. "It will be bad." He thinks many people will leave town. How could they leave their home? But without more jobs, many people would have to leave. Not everyone can farm.

Washington (Main) Street in ▼ 1885

THE DREAM FADES

Still Our Home, 1888

The railroads never came. They passed us by. Without the railroad, Nicodemus stopped growing. Instead, people have been leaving. There is a train station just down the road at Bogue. People moved there.

People moved whole buildings. The bank moved. So did many of the stores. Some people moved their sod homes away brick by brick. Others had their wooden or stone buildings moved. By October, 1888, most of the businesses had closed or moved away.

Nicodemus now looks more like it did when we first arrived. Main Street is empty. But we're not moving. This is our town. We have our own land, and here's where we will stay.

Pa still farms. The weather has been bad. The hotels closed, so Ma helps Pa on the farm. Charles works as a porter on the railroad. He hardly ever comes home.

George Washington has left for Chicago. He promises me he will go to school at night there.

I teach very few children now. Most have moved away. It is sad for me. We all had such dreams for Nicodemus. We still celebrate Emancipation Day. We have food booths, rides, and dancing. Some of the people who left come back. I hope they always will.

It is lonely here, but I still love this town. With Nicodemus, we proved we could stand on our own. I hope people remember that. I think they will.

GLOSSARY

blacksmith – a person who makes things out of iron, such as horseshoes and tools

boomtown – a place that is growing very fast

compass – an instrument for showing directions. A compass has a magnetic needle that points to the north.

county – a unit into which a state is divided for purposes of government

dugout – a rough shelter that is made by digging a hole in the ground

emancipation – being freed from slavery

Exodusters – African Americans who moved from the South to Kansas in the late 1870s

homesteaders – people who settled land given to them by the government

mason – a person who builds with stone or brick

porter – a person who carries baggage

sharecropper – a farmer who gives a share of the crop to the landlord as rent

sod – the top layer of soil that has grass growing on it